X

Poeta en San Francisco | *Barbara Jane Reyes*

X

X

"Winner of the 2005 James Laughlin Award of The Academy of American Poets."
The James Laughlin Award is given to recognize and support a poet's second book. It
is the only second-book award for poetry in the United States. Offered since 1954, the
award was endowed in 1995 by a gift to the Academy from the Drue Heinz Trust. It
is named for the poet and publisher James Laughlin (1914-1997), who founded New
Directions in 1936.

Tinfish Press
Susan M. Schultz, Editor
47-728 Hui Kelu Street #9
Kaneohe, HI 96744

*Tinfish Press is a non-profit, tax-exempt corporation, which supports the publication of
experimental poetry from the Pacific. This project is supported in part by grants from the
State Foundation on Culture and the Arts (SFCA), celebrating over 40 years of culture
and the arts in Hawai`i. The SFCA is funded by appropriations from the Hawai`i State
Legislature and by grants from the NEA.*

www.tinfishpress.com
ISBN# 0-9759376-4-2

Book Design: **Colin Wilkinson/Karen White** Photography: **Michael Relova Price**

[acknowledgments]

Lyrics to "Charlie Don't Surf" © 1980 The Clash.

Thank you/Salamat/Mahalo —

To the editors of the following publications, in which excerpts of *Poeta en San Francisco* have previously appeared, some in earlier versions: *From the Fishouse, Maganda Magazine, MiPoesias, Nocturnes (Re)view, Shifter Magazine, TMP Irregular, Word Riot.*

To those who have provided their critical input and support: Nick Carbo, Jeffery Paul Chan, Oliver de la Paz, Wayne Hangad, Paolo Javier, Daniel Langton, Bino Realuyo, Jose Edmundo Ocampo Reyes, Leny Strobel, Eileen Tabios, and Benito Vergara.

To Oscar Bermeo, for his wonder, and his steadfastness.

I am especially grateful to Stacy Doris for her guidance and mentorship throughout my entire process of writing *Poeta en San Francisco.*

A debt of gratitude to Susan M. Schultz, and many, many thanks to the Academy of American Poets, and to the judges of the 2005 James Laughlin Award: Elizabeth Alexander, James Longenbach, and Susan Stewart.

[table of contents]

[prologue]

[state of emergency]

To honor movement in crescendos of text, combing through ashes for fragments of human bone, studying maps drawn for the absurdity of navigation — what may be so edgy about this state of emergency is my lack of apology for what I am bound to do. For instance, if I dream the wetness of your mouth an oyster my tongue searches for the taste of ocean, if I crave the secret corners of your city on another continent, in another time, in series of circular coils extending outward, then it is only because I continue to harbor the swirls of galaxies in the musculature and viscera of my body. You will appear because I have mouthed your name in half-wish, reluctant to bring myself to you. You will appear for me, because you always do, with earthen skin outside the possibility of human causation.

[asking]

there is ghazal swimming inside of her, wanting to be born. on the
matter of foretelling, of small miracles, cactus flowers in bloom on
this city fire escape, where inside your tongue touches every inch of
her skin, where you lay your hand on her belly and sleep. here, she
fingers the ornate remains of ancient mosques. here, some mythic
angel will rise from the dust of ancestors' bones. this is where you
shall worship, at the intersections of distilled deities and memory's
sharp edges. the country is quite a poetic place; water and rock
contain verse and metaphor, even wild grasses reply in rhyme. you are
not broken. she knows this having captured a moment of lucidity;
summer lightning bugs, sun's rays in a jelly jar.

this is not a love poem, but a cove to escape the flux, however
momentary. she is still a child, confabulating the fantastic; please do
not erode her wonder for the liquid that is your language. there is
thunderstorm in her chest, wanting to burst through her skin. this is
neither love poem nor plea. this is not river, nor stone.

(ə-pŏk'ə-lĭ-ps')

n.

dear love is it true there are no demons but the ones we've invented
fallen from firmament's edges into oceans of fire harnessed splintering
secrecy's epidemic trace salt circles upon stone virgins' breached
fortresses mercy aversion

tell me your name awakens carved flesh sutures continue to pray once
the word is uttered the sky will open its thunder because doubt was
never cast

no memory corroborates   we exiles in the register of baptism.

dear love, i cannot remember when we last spoke.

[poeta en san francisco]

"El Camino Real ends here."
—*Alejandro Murguía, "16th & Valencia"*

[orient]

consider this procession:

wings of black paloma dispersing and capturing air,
babies in the costumes of cherubs,
la virgen de guadalupe on a float of roses,
a weeping siren, a brothel girl.

we find ourselves retracing the steps of gold
hungry arrogant spaniards. walking on knees
behind their ghosts, could we ever know how
much blood has seeped into the soil —
this church, a prison. here, tongues
severed and fed to wild animals.

en esta ciudad we have forgotten how to speak.

aquí, en esta ciudad sin memoria,
where padres roped indians vaquero-style,
dropped their corpses into unmarked graves
after searing and coveting bare flesh —

i learned how to say the rosary with these scented beads,
amber rosebuds, pressed into my face, forming silent
alliances with outcasts and expatriates, street corner
denizens, old women veiled with black lace, murmuring
benediction under fake gothic arches and ebony crosses.

in my native tongue, breath is word is spirit.
i can think of no single, adequate translation.

the opposite of eden:

we are penned in this narrow strip of land,
sutured by train tracks and high voltage wire,
where these piss and dank stankin alleys
embrace and tear us from our vigilance —
without so much as a sustainable gospel.

in our collisions, we learn to make new:
from our lacerated and fractured selves,
appendages resembling tails, horns.
and, siempre, wings to capture breath.

"The pure products of America go crazy."

en esta ciudad, where homeless 'nam vets
wave old glory and pots for spare change;
she grows weary of the daily routine:

fuckinjapgobacktochina!
allthemfuckingooknamessoundthesame!

and especially:
iwasstationedatsubicbay.

aquí, en las calles de esta ciudad,
they pray their tropical dreams will come
true again: blow jobs under a sticky table.
cheaper than a pint of watered down beer.
they want to touch her. on their greasy lips,

maganda ka mahal kita magkano ka

and if she believed in God,
and if her tongue had not been severed,
then she could issue this damnation:

wala kang pag-asa pag darating ang araw ng pahayag

A fiery archangel brings this message,
a prophecy of battle for the end of time.
There are demons among our ranks,
my love. We could have had their wings,
their crimson, leathery wings. And claws,
glistening, to hold each other tight.

En La Misión, between earth and sky,
at crossroads, we are vigilant, poised
with trumpets and warrior blades.
Among the tombstones, a glade
of heaven hides. Beneath our boots,
murky water rushes to the sea.

The weeping siren's lesions and track marks
have cleared her memory of oceantide.
See the clouds gather in her gelatin eyes.

If she could have only run away from here.

Apocalypse, she's been told,
is the ending of *this*, the beginning of *that*.
Etymology informs her it is an uncovering.

Church of the severed tongues,
church of the whispering, hollowed men,
church of desire, spasm, descent,
church of the scourged, of those with no name,
church of paralyzed voice, church of violent soul,
church of the sightless, church of broken glass,

To thee we pray with baited breath —
Bring the darkness. Let the darkness come.

dear love,

remember the bamboo tiger cages in those goddamn movies. and
napalm, sinister rain, deathly tangerine vapor veiling the islands, for
simulation's nothing like the real thing. the real thing. the real thing.
military choppers of film script, steel demon birds, called away to
quell real life dictatorship's farthest outposts of rebellion. who among
us could've told the difference? they have mistaken my home for a
hollywood set of your home. even my language was a stand-in for
yours. your country is not a war. my country is no longer mine. this i
wished to tell you, because i was thinking of coming home to you.

yours.

[the victory prayer]

lord almighty, our young killing machines wave stars and stripes in battle cry. let medals gleam upon their chests for their valor. father all knowing, let our spirits dwell in them as they smite our enemies. father, help them, help us, to bear the stench of our enemies' bodies blown asunder by our thunder of bombs, in your name.

lord, make us steel against their pleas for mercy as we crumble their homes, their infidel wives, their devil offspring. lord, let us decimate their land, let them languish in their own waste, in your name.

let them beg for swift death, and force upon them long suffering instead. lamb of god, take away all of their hope. father in heaven, let them weep rivers unending.

and if our boys should perish lord, let them die most nobly. we ask you, our source of love, knowledge, and refuge, to take them into your kingdom. our father protector, for humble victory, in your name, we sing alleluiah.

Aquí, en mi ciudad de sueños,
I missed the parades this week.
Maré, forgive me, for
I closed my eyes instead.
Under the weight of Old Glory,
stooped old men stooping lower
than I thought possible.
I couldn't bear the sight of it.
Between decreed days of honor,
you think of their faces, twisting,
blood clots in the brain. Today,
you pretend they are your heroes.

El valiente, el nómada.
La sangre, las venas, la ruptura.

Consider this procession:

Those missing pieces of themselves,
held up by will, metal stilts,
antiquated wheelchairs.
Quad-pod canes if they've got
adequate health insurance.
Amputation's romance, enacted
upon world stages. Videotaped.
Everywhere, that fucking flag.
Phantasms of ticker tape.
Funereal brass mimicking festiveness.

Día de los muertos.

Those who fought with only scythes and sticks,
those who have held their innards in with a pot lid,
they are not present and accounted for here.

Sin ofrendas. Sin oración.
Desaparecido.

[kundiman]

they call the river goddess whore
deflower bayonet stillbirth fertile

she gathers wind in her skirts
escaping ascension opens a world

they peruse local obituaries
foreign concepts natural causes

she gathers collateral damage
headlines prophecy cycles of birth

[objet d'art: exhibition of beauty in art loft victorian claw tub]

he found her, guttered, fish-hook positioned. palsied arms squeezing
mottled fishtail he thought almost fetal. febrile she felt his face
eclipsed sun his halo at best. joyless, cradled old faerie tale, this half-
dead thing little foundling. but city rain gutters' unspeakable odors,
her hair matted nest of gems and dying creatures. he wrapped her
in newspaper he brought her home traced spider veins' routes where
needles went in islands of abscess where flesh refused to mend itself.
he suspected she had no navel. he put his hand there to find what else
she lacked.

she has no memory now, the order in which events transpired: deposit
specimen laid porcelain bed iodine smarting contusions expensive
soles clicking waxed hardwood renovated rocksalt bathwater
proportions tested flashbulb popping ceaseless yellow afterimage
sandalwood combs fighting ebony tangles exquisite centerpiece
erupting stomach's detoxification applause and eyes always eyes offset
against vaulted ceilings she does not remember singing.

[esta semana santa]

it is the season of penitence worshipping white messiah our village
boys do esta cuaresma the church turns away we chant because the
city man who owns our rice fields demands more and more so our
boys whip their backs leather tipped with sharp metals their field
worn palms blood lashed five-inch iron nails dipped in alcohol
just few moments hanging good show say flashbulbs popping
sunburnt white people barely hold down their lunches they weep
these people are barbaric how does it come to this so sad they point
digicamcorders sad bleeding boys

haven't we always captivated travelers and social voyeurs black
saturday soul searching redemption of scattered flocks epic-singing
on all continents in a language our children no longer recognize
otherwise our villages are quaint

just quiet, and quaint.

[diwata taga ilog at dagat]

regarding the turbulent south seas, the sultan stages elaborate
ceremony. as if one man could wed a goddess, part woman, part ocean.

elders say when she walked on earth, her skin's sores and scales a
jealous woman's curse upon her, a maiden who escaped betrothal to
a wicked deity. a rice farmer's daughter who found death before her
time, she found river dolphins kindred.

elders say she loves moonstone, polished jade. elders say her penchant
for mischief, elders say she preys.

elders say when ships, when the nailed god came, his hairy men
christened her demon. they forbade her offerings. they erected bamboo
fences in the shallows. still the elders whisper, sometimes sing.

> *when undertow captures foolish boy,*
> *lotus flower petals in monsoon.*
>
> *when she finds he is not to her liking,*
> *lotus flower feast for typhoon.*

[hulaan]

she wonders why the sea behaves
so strangely; today, its stillness
unnerves her. she knows that it's
unusual for the tide to dip so low,
exposing seabed's skeletons,
ships whose hulls once bellowed
                    whalesong, lost souls.

today, boys hop out of outrigger
canoes to gather shells and fish;
flopping in ancient mud, they fill
their rattan vessels. tonight, oceanside
fires will burn and crackle, and she
will divine still air's smoke curls.
                    something is amiss.

dear love, the time is near.

seven churches' testimonies witness exiles. a beast whose voice is
water. angels walk among wicked apostles, enticing morningstar's
church of liars. angel of the city descends. the door opens carnelian
and emerald. elders' lightning seas of glass sing holy, holy. worthy are
the slain. praise measures deeds.

the souls of martyrs wail, how long, how long.

dear love, i turn my face your lips graze my cheek i smell nicotine on
your breath you told me you quit what wells up inside me wishes to
shut herself down please understand. please.   understand.

wait, black sun. wait, blood moon. wait, dear love.

From the streetcorner's beat up boombox:

Charlie don't surf and we think he should
Charlie don't surf and you know that it ain't no good
Charlie don't surf for his hamburger Momma
Charlie's gonna be a napalm star

And I laugh at the coincidence,
because up until yesterday
(I am embarrassed to say),
I did not know who Charlie was,
mistook him for GI slang for some
US Airborne Cavalry Division's
blond American killing machine,
a freckled boy from the landlocked
middle of this country, homecoming
king and all star quarterback,
who'd knocked up his girl in a barn
or in the back of a beat up Chevy,
who'd never seen beyond cornfields
until crouched eye to eye,
machine gun to machete,
with his slanty-eyed animal enemy
in some malarial jungle —

The opposite of Eden.

He inhabited a blank landmass on my map;
and that is why I thought Charlie don't surf.

dear love, we make plans, and we rescind. stars fall as figs in the wind. call to the mountains, four winds held by angels. call to land and sea, so let it be. praise be to blood of lambs, tearless, opening silence in heaven. offer hands of fire to bitter rivers. eagles lament locusts with human faces, lions' teeth, sulfur breastplates, scorpion tails.

dear love, abysmal angel, for sightless idols robed in cloud. even prophets' words can sour. great city streets lined by the fallen for all to gaze upon before breath collapses, glorifies. the woman clothed in sun births a serpent's feast. earth opens its mouth to swallow the serpent's river. miracles and signs, boombox and bling bling.

dear love, this calls for wisdom.

[prayer to angry gods]

Charlie don't surf he'll never learn
Charlie don't surf though he's got a gun
Charlie don't surf think that he should
Charlie don't surf we really think he should

and up the street, the basilica
shines god's golden smile.
it is the season of sacrifice,
and far across the ocean,
penitents scourge their bodies.
the surrogate christ prepares
hands and feet for holy week.
he will take the nails to his own flesh.

and deeper into the jungle's heart,
devoted prostrate facing mecca.
they took their enemies' heads,
as was the custom before nailed
gods visited these shores. they took
heads, not long ago. they take heads
now, and missionaries still believe
conversion can save their necks.

[Kumintang]

That blank space on your map, that's where I was born.
The more blank your map, the more darkness for exploration.

Gold stars pinned to your chest for every military and civilian
slaughter, for every child defiled, for every rice field set ablaze,
for every leveled village, for every racial slur coined
in these blank spaces on your map, for every new howling
wilderness, for every incineration of flesh, for every gasoline
victory smell in the morning. Counting kill, your body is lost.
There is no hope for your spirit. Don't try. Shit. Don't dream.

Can you appreciate the neither here nor there of it all?
Think how soft now, your rot of a body. Your fucking filth.
Blood and whiskey, some homecoming.

[why choose pilipinas?]

the answer is simple, dear ally. the pilipinas are the finest group of
islands in the world, its strategic position unexcelled by that of any
other global positioning. they afford means of protecting american
interests which, with the very least output of physical power, have
the effect of commanding position for hostile action.

he who promises to return, repeatedly returns. ankle-deep in his
reflection pool, his bronze statue smokes a good bronze corncob pipe.

his commander-in-chief self-names doctrine: headquarter force
containment of communism. the pilipinas play key logistical roles
supporting service fulcrums of american indochina penetration. fleets
and stations deploy venereal disease; deflowered local catholics satiate
battalions, all vietnam bound. in short, the pilipinas are custom
tailored to fit your diverse needs.

[why choose pilipinas, remix]

the answer is simple, my friend. pilipinas are noteworthy for their
beauty, grace, charm. they are especially noted for their loyalty. their
nature is sun sweetened. their smiles downcast, coy. pilipinas possess
intrinsic beauty men find delightful and irresistible. pilipinas are
family-oriented by essence, resourceful, devoted. what's more, english
is the true official language of the pilipinas, so communication is
uncomplicated. and even though some believe in the old ways,
the majority of the pilipinas are christian, so you are assured they
believe in the one true god you do. foreign, but not too foreign, they
assimilate quickly and they do not make a fuss. in short, the pilipinas
are custom tailored to fit your diverse needs.

now will that be cash or charge?

[dis • orient]

(nū, nyū)
adj.

as in, make it...

what suits this era of technological violence.
what genteel traditions of his own unremembered.
what terrible excitement of catastrophic revolutions.
what pound appropriation of the ancient oriental.
what avant garde experiment carves her lover's flesh.

[he we a piki te pi pi so
a sayi we sa we gi ba to o koti
he we a bika we ha te ki ni po o pomi
we ha no kopo beka o te mongo
we go te su pe su
we anio sa rito te oti a po o sodo
sodopo mi sodo i su we a hogi a tisi
o depi i no yi ma so no o ka li he pi detu
we go ti o pi so
we sa we we be le tu ba i otobi
ti i no i i doya apa we ha no kopo]

1. not previously encountered

silken forms from far east slice china melons.
silent sylphs, sampaguita and seaspray aromas
wafting. of jade gardens, terraced mountainsides,
bamboo thickets, some primordial magic,
some concealed eden awaits his cartography.

ᜂ ᜐᜓᜇᜓ ᜁ ᜊᜒᜆᜒ ᜊᜓ ᜏᜒ ᜏᜓ ᜈᜓ ᜇᜆᜓ ᜆᜓ ᜂ ᜃᜓᜆᜒ
ᜏ ᜉᜓᜏᜒ ᜑ ᜃᜓ ᜁᜆᜓ ᜊᜓᜐᜓ
ᜏᜓ ᜃᜇᜒᜂ ᜆᜒ ᜄᜒᜈᜒᜇ
ᜑᜓᜐᜒ ᜑᜒ ᜑᜓᜐᜒ ᜁᜊᜒ ᜀ ᜆᜒᜇᜒ ᜆᜒ ᜏᜒ ᜐᜓ
ᜏᜒ ᜑ ᜈᜓ ᜇᜒ ᜆᜒ ᜊᜆᜒ ᜀ ᜋᜓ
ᜊᜒ ᜑᜒᜊᜒ ᜑᜒ ᜑᜓᜐᜒ ᜀ ᜆᜒᜇᜒ
ᜆᜒ ᜄᜒᜈᜒᜇ ᜀ ᜂ ᜆᜒ ᜆᜒ ᜐᜓᜇᜒ ᜀ ᜊᜒ ᜆᜒ
ᜆᜒ ᜑᜓᜐᜒ ᜀ ᜏᜒ ᜆ ᜆᜒ ᜄᜒᜈᜒᜇ ᜑ ᜁᜊᜓᜇᜒ ᜀᜇᜓ ᜀ ᜃᜓᜏᜒᜊᜒ ᜂᜈᜋᜒᜆᜒ ᜏᜒ ᜉᜒ ᜐᜒ
ᜆᜒ ᜁᜈᜒᜋᜒ ᜁ ᜐᜒ ᜏᜒ ᜋᜓ ᜊᜒ ᜃᜇᜒᜉᜓ
ᜏᜒ ᜏᜒ ᜐᜒ ᜂ ᜆᜒ ᜏᜒᜎᜓ ᜏᜒ ᜇᜓᜉᜒ ᜏᜒ ᜐᜒ
ᜏᜒ ᜃᜓ ᜊ ᜁ ᜆᜒ ᜐᜓ
ᜏᜒ ᜄᜓ ᜐᜓᜎᜒ ᜏᜒ ᜀ ᜑᜓᜄᜒ ᜀ ᜆᜒᜐᜒ
ᜂ ᜋᜒ ᜁ ᜉᜓ ᜂ ᜐᜓᜇᜓ ᜏᜓ ᜏᜒ ᜃᜓ ᜂ ᜂ ᜄᜒ

[o sodo i biti bo we wo no dato to o koti
wa powi ha ko itu boso
wo kadiu te ginida
hosi he hosi ibi a tidi ti we so
we ha no di te bati a mu
be hibi hi hosi a tidi
te ginida a o te te sodi a be te
te hosi a we ta te ginida ha ibudi adu a kuwibi onamiti we pi si
te inimi i se we mo be kadipu
we we si o ti wilo we dupi we si
we ko ba i te so
we go soli we a hugi a tisi
o mi i po o sodo wo wi ku o o gi]

2. never used before now

the scribe expresses profound disillusion —
the edifices of his own empire are lackluster.
he tastes others' tongues and tang so curious,
so fresh, he discovers they are to his liking.
he names himself sage eradicator of ennui.

[we yilo go a we diyiwi we pa po so a lati a we we du po mo o mo
pogiti te ki a pisi

itilidiyi mi ka diti i po ti si a po ti wi bodi a we te a we yu ipisali te wa
noti a ko popo a te ma noti o si kosi o o mota kosi i uli te ko be o ta
pilosi a we a so o o he a mi a wiu digi

a te i wa si o tu so wa soti i ladi go a yu to ti no o dako hoko te we ha
noti bu tu a mimodi i komu]

3. just arrived

a fool, he believes his boots to be the first
markers of civilization. women, bare-breasted,
offer fragrant garlands. lovely, their smiles,
their thick rivers of henna ebony hair.
pintada, he calls them for their tinted skins.

[a te we sipadatu ha ko to i wo we mi a tabo itu sidiyu to a ti titisi po
o ti tuni a titi wati ito a bali o ti tosa bi puwi ta wa ti pi bali a itu te
tosa bali po o bosi a piwi

a we sibi hani a di o go o ka te i ka poma a he kopani

a te ka a asu te tuma o siyu to mi mi payi o a diyiwi mo oga]

4. changed for the better

for every daemonic place he erects stone
archangels and infernos, exacts penance
from those driven underground, spills his seed,
his battle cry, his body presses firm dispensation.
he invents himself by extracting others' titles.

[a yu wo wa o wi mi to te witi kuni o te kati to te dinati tipi we wati
abu i ki a bo diya we bo puti a te sa o mo oga a du we dipi li dagosa
gui ga gi o te wati pisu lati we kutisa gui a komi wio hida we te wilu
pa pali li so a te bimilo gi giti do abu sosi a te wati a hadi pi di dipiti
gi ibu ibu pati gi a a pi si i yu moli gapuli pati a te gi singi ba a i oti
dasi i tapai buka a te we liti te sa a itidoti i tusi i o odi te ko

a a te ko to a i

a i no aga to be me we]

5. recently obtained or acquired

wives from cherry blossoms catalogues and bars adjacent
to military bases. black market handguns, .45 caliber
samurais and angels. assault rifles nicknamed "shorty."
sexy clandestine WMD's. means of acquisition not in
question free enterprise as cyclical self-reinvention.

ᤖ ᤖ ᤗ ᤖ ᤖ ᤖ ᤖ ᤖ ᤖ ᤖ ᤖ
ᤗ ᤖ ᤖ ᤖ ᤗ ᤖ ᤖ ᤗ
ᤗ ᤖ ᤖ ᤖ ᤖ ᤖ ᤗ ᤖ
ᤗ ᤖ ᤖ ᤖ ᤖ ᤗ ᤖ ᤖ ᤖ ᤗ
ᤖ ᤖ ᤖ ᤖ ᤖ ᤖ ᤖ ᤖ ᤖ ᤖ
ᤖ ᤖ ᤗ ᤖ ᤖ ᤖ ᤖ

ᤖ ᤗ ᤖ ᤖ ᤖ ᤖ ᤗ
ᤖ ᤖ ᤖ ᤖ ᤖ
ᤖ ᤖ ᤖ ᤖ ᤖ ᤖ ᤖ ᤖ
ᤖ ᤖ ᤖ ᤖ ᤖ ᤖ ᤖ ᤖ ᤖ

[we mi ha wa si ku sa ako mi puhi
pa i abo te po ga poli powi
yu ka bi o babo si payi hosi
yu wa abo mi si payi wi te bo po
a we we o libi i ti bilagi o koka
tu sa pipo wiu rili o sopisu

a poti i madi mi lo yu
i nibi la bii bapu
luwii mi hi i loku a te wa
kali to a tusa ti i nibi luki ba]

6. strikingly unusual

because she found nascence entering his field of view.
because his words lay waste to her disparaged homeland.
because he posited her simply as his other.
because he invoked her, a muse for signification.
because casualties of war are a necessary expenditure.

[a piti i sopi soli
i desede mi do to be migi wi yu
pudibi a pudibi a pudibi
we so i ki ti lo o

a siti yu dipati
yu we ito pa kotoyi be dibi o sidi idi
a yu ha be go po pe mo
te moki ma sodopu nosi obihi]

7. latest in sequence

please understand, if she does not tug at your heart strings,
then you will not see truths in her testimony. if you do not
believe your wars have ever assaulted her splintered form,
her fissured tribes, then you will not acknowledge her
as anything other than a cheaply constructed replica of you.

[yu dagi yu pi we yu we o
be ti ga no ti mo i go dipidi musi
to di to ki ti awa
te libi pa ili i atu i we
te paadi butipi a adidi yilu we agu
ubi te ga i te we gadi
te ho mi i go odi
i yu a komi do to te nado o te dibi kia
pisi li mi ko bipodiha
a i we ko o to mi yu
                a pa a kopusa]

8. currently fashionable

he speaks words that were never his to speak.
he speaks words that were never his to speak.
he speaks words that were never his to speak.
he speaks words that were never his to speak.
he does not know the gravity of such offense.

ᜢ ᜲ ᜲ ᜳ ᜡ ᜮ ᜢᜢ ᜮ3
ᜢ ᜲ ᜲᜲ ᜮ ᜲ ᜢᜲ
ᜢ ᜲ ᜲ ᜮ ᜲ ᜲ ᜱ ᜢ
ᜡ ᜳ ᜳ ᜲ ᜲ ᜲᜢ ᜮᜲ
ᜢ ᜲ 3 ᜢᜲ ᜲ ᜲ ᜲ ᜲ
ᜢ ᜡ ᜮ ᜲ ᜧ ᜲ ᜲ ᜡ
ᜲ ᜢ ᜲ ᜲ ᜮ ᜢᜡ
ᜡ ᜳ 3 ᜳ ᜲ 3 ᜢ
ᜲ ᜲ ᜡ ᜢᜲ ᜡᜲ 3

[i ma a pa we yu era pou
i ha ditete yu lo inu
i ko to yu a a go ki
wo ha ha a pi hidi pati
i a o inu no to ma pi
i wa yu ta bo ti ni wo
no i a ti po kabi
we ha o sa a o ro
li te be komi beti o]

dear love, when you speak of war and memory, bulletsong. what do i know of war? dead butterflies fall out of my mouth when you speak of suffering, how you tire of it.

dear love, you are not my love. you're an emblem, and sometimes a trophy. and sometimes a trope. this street is not yours and the sooner i dissociate you from here the sooner will my war obsession end.

[a compendium of angels]

angel of blades beating air synthetic sound chemical rain blood sunset
pearls steel demon birds vapor rising jungle's fire trees erase the name
of here. blades twirl inverted faces. orange sky fallen cities of broken
stone. awakened into nothing, comforted by shards, memory can be
filled with so much detonation.

angel of descent's interlocked confessions. angel of black smoke air
raid sirens. heaven is infected wound attack formation sun rising
missile dance skimming the skin of ocean.

angel of morphine's shrapnel embedded in flesh. jet fighters needle sea spume's virgin gowns. the opposite of home, this gun-happy necessity. in labor camps, women strap explosives to their bodies and unfurl wings in ululation. the river parts its waters.

angel of rock and roll first world impotence, ordered to leave no evidence. despite this, the dead still hang from trees. parched, earth drinks.

angel of autumn patrol ambush upriver clarity clean genocide. she
climbs coffins so that she will not sleep, hides bullets in baskets of
rice. she barters fuel drums for me love you long time. she blows
bridges disney electric light show in the asshole of the world.
liberators rebuild and she blows them up again.

angel of racial epithet, your enemy is a dismembered fuck you in the
wind. snipers collect tusks of wild boar, go native. angel of corrugated
metal shacks, steel vessels spectral bodies swallowed, lulled by jungle.

angel of machetes, stone dragon sentinels, even corpses must
be guarded, for skulls and souls find a way back to their gods.
how lovesong is contracted from "if it were not so," holds
relevance, especially here, where buzzing malaria bamboo prisons
are no mythology.

angel of proper burials, let earth and river reclaim their fractured
children. adorned in violet ribbons, we mimic predatory birds'
movements beating brass gongs.

angel of heathen incantation, a procession of painted headhunters crosses international borders. adolescents wield scythes and semiautomatic rifles. a child's third eye opens with a diamond bullet. headdressed elders invoke river spirits. bend the imagination, and the landscape is dotted charred crucifixion.

the opposite of eden: angel of guerrilla resistance, let typhoon deities conceal your tattered soldiers. let ceremonies of rain and fire measure the weight of the final kill.

[palabras y notas para el viajero]

calle de la fundación

the people small ethnic gender illusion catwalk because few speak
english ubiquitous oriental excellent at cutting fish otherworld
packaged fiery hot longlife cater to delicious mingling convenience
gizmos edging carved jesus reprimanding mankind and the self well-
manicured movie-going ultra-rich vestibules gilded cloisonné rooftop
peacock ersatz psychedelia influx of hard drugs advertise nightlife
detour across incongruous grey cement galleon memorial gate

separating worlds on the altar resides heaven an interesting conjecture
of prostitutes poets 3-eyed gods of smoke always on the right alleys
proliferate transcontinental merchants flood xenophobia alliances

[galleon prayer]
pilipinas to petatlán

she whispers desert trees, thorn-ridged, trickling yellow candles; roots
    spilling snakes' blood
virgin of ribboned silk; virgin of gold filigree
one day's walk westward, a crucifix of fisherman's dinghy dimensions
    washes ashore
virgin adorned in robe of shark embryo and coconut husk
she fingers mollusks, wraps herself in sea vines
virgin of ocean voyage peril
she wills herself born
virgin of mud brick ruins; virgin of sandstorm echoes
she is saint of commonplaces; saint of badlands
virgin of jade, camphor, porcelain; virgin of barter for ghosts
penitents, earthdivers of forgotten names praying skyward
virgin of scars blossomed from open veins of fire
she slips across the pacific's rivers of pearldiving children
virgin of copper coins
she is bloodletting words, painting unlikeness
virgin of anachronism
children stained with berries and rust, their skeletons bend, arrow-tipped;
    smoke blurs eyes' edges
virgin of mineral depletion; virgin of mercury
at other altitudes she remembers to breathe; a monument scraping cloud
virgin of tin deposits extracted from mountains
these are not divinations; there is goldleaf about her skin
virgin of naming and renaming places in between

plaza del burguesía americano

north of market's upscale shopping mecca's center you can't miss the
huge female personification of victory riding an erect 97-foot granite
phallus to commemorate commodore dewey's victory over the spanish
armada in manila bay on may 1, 1898 this monument dedicated by
gun totin' fist shakin' rough rider teddy on may 14, 1903 to end a
splendid little war to begin what is known as a small insurrection

iglesia de los immigrantes pobres

located across the street from gentrification's central edifice the irish
saint's church intersects calle de la misión founded to minister the
city's growing gold starved earthquakes could not crumble the faith
of the devout and the city landmarked subsequent seismic retrofits
today's pilipinos replace yesterday's irish such gothic interior even a
stigmatic would feel at home here

[prayer of the banished]

We've been told to keep the strangers out
We don't like them starting to hang around
We don't like them all over town
Across the world we are going to blow them down

hail holy queen mother of mercy
our life our sweetness our final hope
we who are banished daughters of eve weep penitents' tears
we fill these alleys with our tears we flood these streets
and pray that downward will your gracious eyes gaze
that we exiles may know redemption
our lady of sorrow and commiseration
holy mother of god blessed mother of the word
merciful mother loving mother pray for us

under freeway overpass sunday worship
congregation's shopping carts sleeping bags
whiskey in paper sacks nothing to eat
a teenage runaway wonders if tonight
will be the night she will sleep unmolested

j-town

even the sidewalk's evocative of isamu noguchi sculpture gardens
this part of town is sanitary he thinks so refined he has come for
cherry blossoms fluttering his eyelashes for the way of incense and of
tea roseate cheeked beauties whose almond eyes whose hair spun silk
glow midnight hues giggle at him and hide their faces from his
pocket dictionary he reads konnichiwa bends at the waist they giggle
some more

genmaichai brews in glazed vessels bearing hand-painted ideographs
slid shut behind rice paper screens poised upon tatami mats fragrance
of bamboo quickens his pulse luminous her skin she kneels and
spreads he breathes and savors salted plum sweetness blooming on
his tongue

breaking bliss roars the 38 down geary past land water fire wind sky
of the peace pagoda he exhales and the giggling girls with almond
eyes find pucca funny love dolls and forget all about him

[exaltation of the lowly]

lord, make me your instrument, bringer of all light for i no longer see,
these days so disconsolate. lord, i am your vessel. do unto me and have
done as is your will and your word.

beneath the black moon, she eats flowers for their powdery perfume.
in her memory's opiate haze, crouching days of only swamp cabbage,
sleepless beneath palm fronds during monsoon, when thick tongued
men pumped grandfather and elder brother full of lead, dragged
mother away pleading. this, the price of liberation.

blade slit force once tore open her thighs. this, the price of youth and
piety. then, crumbled cathedrals' tarnished eucharist, even spaniard
arrogance could not withstand constant aerial bombardment. native
girls stolen away in the night, bartered for bootleg booze and black
market cigarettes. now, her granddaughter cowers beneath the peace
pagoda. now he preys.

father, i am emptied. father, hear me.

c-town

he'll have none of this amputated 'nam vet whose only words are
hellfire and oriental pussy whose only friend is a 22 oz clear bottle of
king cobra bought for 93 cents grit and stink of portsmouth square
chattering bent men pigeon shit on everything here ducks hang
upside down in windows feet and heads and beaks and eyes here
beauties are gems in dung heaps somehow ni hao always gets stuck in
his throat

[the sorrowful mystery]

she forgives those who trespass *as it was in the beginning* this corrido(r)
city sliver splintered here hymns processional appease the people
seething shards of ancestors remain here   still
so shall it be again

m-town

he is wondering if there are hot chicks in m-town he is wondering
what in god's name m-town stands for he's never heard of it before
the only thing he must know is that m-town is a ghost its inhabitants
grow old they wait

calle de sección ocho, casas de abuelos y de abuelas

the unused hole in the ground located at the corner of kearny and
jackson across from celluloid god's patina café may one day contain
supportive tenant services and artifacts of blue men's billy clubs in the
meantime just gawk at it and take polaroids don't hold your breath
few descend into the hole it's been 30 years

to unbind yourself from chainlink to descend into the hole to
commune with ghosts and discarded things to pray that chinatown's
pagoda curves will misdirect the exiled dead from returning

[ave maria]

our lady who crushes serpents
our lady of lamentation
our lady full of grace whose weeping statues bleed,
our lady who makes the sun dance, pray for us

our lady of salt pilgrimage
our lady of building demolition
our lady of crack houses
santa maría, madre de dios, pray for us sinners

our lady of unbroken hymen
preteen vessel of god's seed,
your uterus is a blessed receptacle.

our lady of neon strip joints
our lady of blowjobs in kerouac alley
our lady of tricked out street kids, pray for us

blessed mother of cholo tattoos
you are the tightest homegirl

our lady of filas and lipliner
our lady of viernes santo procession
our lady of garbage-sifting toothless men
our lady of urban renewal's blight

pray for us sinners   ipanalangin n'yo kaming makasalanan
now and at the hour   ngayon at kung
of our death   kami ay mamamatay

amen

calle de los orientales

mapped cosmopolitan mudflats marshland in former lifetimes
intersecting accident memory and an island named for angels
tantalize voyeurs alleyways accessible portions aromatic bowing
iconoclast clotheslines waving substandard influx conspire private
rice enticing ancient often misidentified and always *italicized*
exotic heart of here

do not be disconcerted that they do not speak english they might
as well be from another planet just point to indicate what you
want or what looks good and they will do (it for) you with a smile

Lord. Have mercy. Christ. Have mercy.
Lord. Have mercy. Christ. Hear us.
Christ. Can you hear us?

Whoever the fuck is up there —
Have mercy on us. Have mercy on us.
Have mercy on us. Have mercy on us.

Holy Mary, pray for us.
Holy Mother of God, pray for us.
Holy Virgin of virgins, pray for us.
Mother of appropriated Christ, pray for us.
Mother of Hypocrites' Church, pray for us.
Mother of Divine Punishment, pray for us.
Mother most pure, pray for us.
Mother most chaste, pray for us.
Mother inviolate, pray for us.
Mother undefiled, pray for us.
Mother most silent, pray for us.
Mother most compliant, pray for us.
Mother of severed tongues, pray for us.
Mother of the captured, pray for us.
Mother of our betrayal, pray for us.

calle de comidas exóticas

turo-turo meaning point-point joints present styrofoam bowls of
tamarind soup oxtails tripe peanut stew *dinuguan* (that's chocolate
meat to you) cellophane coconut milk sticky displayed silent
women glass encased to service you though not for the weak-willed
this is an adventure you shouldn't pass up!

do not dip your hands into fish sauce fermented shrimp paste
vessels do not grimace tasting salty wetness do not forget to clean
up your own mess here no frills leaving gratuity is customary mark
of manners

Virgin most prudent, pray for us.
Virgin most disembodied, pray for us.
Virgin most self-denied, pray for us.
Virgin most unquestioning, pray for us.
Virgin most desexed, pray for us.
Virgin most impalpable, pray for us.
Mirror of technological violence, pray for us.
Seat of warmongers' rhetoric, pray for us.
Cause of our naiveté, pray for us.
Spiritual vessel, pray for us.
Singular vessel of insemination, pray for us.
Mystical deflowering, pray for us.
Tower of the Almighty Dollar, pray for us.
Tower of bruised women, pray for us.
House of gold-hungry rapists, pray for us.
Locked Gate of Heaven, pray for us.
Morningstar, pray for us.
Health of trick turners, pray for us.
Refuge of venereal disease, pray for us.
Comforter of dumpster divers, pray for us.
Help of Christian killing machines, pray for us.

calle del consejo práctico

do not be deceived by ethnic ghetto zest's barhop and boogie use
reasonable caution when walking unsavory districts for kicky dining
amongst lush and plush urbanoids, kooky and kitschy, freewheeling
trendoids for even the moneyed sport funk-to-grunge artsy attire.

calle de los morenos

make sure you understand well this neighborhood's charming
blend of latin turf war and martini bars in stilettos and a cocktail
dress you cannot run from their eyes avoid dark side streets and
always avoid speaking to dark men on sidewalks when they holla
hola chula chinita japonesa

calle de la oscuridad

do not give 'nam vets change or cigarettes hold your purse close to
your breast (clasp facing inward) some do not have legs so you can
rest assured they will not follow you if you walk quickly past them
hold your breath but do not make it obvious

Queen of fallen angels, pray for us.
Queen of patriarchs, pray for us.
Queen of dictators, pray for us.
Queen of race riots, pray for us.
Queen of heathens' torched flesh, pray for us.
Queen of tortured prisoners, pray for us.
Queen of virgins sold into sex trade, pray for us.
Queen of teenage whores sniffin glue, pray for us.
Queen of slumlords, pray for us.
Queen of smack crack and blow, pray for us.
Queen of cardboard shelters, pray for us.
Queen of gold-toothed pimps, pray for us.
Queen of cigar and rope burns, pray for us.

Pray for us, O Holy Mother of God.
That we may be worthy.
Pray for us.
That we may be.
Pray for us.
That we may.
Pray.

calles de los dolores y trastorno de tensión postraumática

your methods are unacceptable :: beyond human restraint :: things
get confused i know :: the heart's a white sepulcher and no man
guards its doors :: against the growing dark :: incessant blades beat
air :: incessant blades :: what means are available to terminate :: gook
names :: with extreme prejudice :: you may use those :: blades beat
:: easier than learning their gook names :: your boys don't know any
better than :: gook names :: dead men hanging from trees so far from
the known world :: how does it come to this :: being blown to hell
:: incessant :: gook names :: in panic mode trigger finger instinct
efficiency :: incessant blades beat air :: blades beat :: dead men
hanging :: gook names :: no sin committed :: no dead men ::
to forgive.

[assumption]

she laid down
on the train tracks.
brown girl — maybe
seventeen. sparkly

shoelaces, all that
was left. girlfriend
wasn't doin no drugs.
just gave up is all.

the morning paper
reported a suicide —
filipina crack whore,
nothing to live for.

[re • orient]

[uyayi]

in the dream the bubble where there is no time not in the way you
or i understand it moves in the dream things are veiled and this veil
makes time creep and oftentimes stand still ghosts' dusty costumes
of medals gleam for defenses breached territories conquered in the
dream bodies river buoys make the noise of women bathing

she thinks of the stream running underground she remembers a
fable of sarongs unknotted at river's edges tricksters hiding in the
mangroves women who so loved the sound of water rushing that the
gods   transformed them

[prayer to san francisco de asís]

the brothel girl in the mirror coos back at me.
she reminds me not to curse her ill fate, for
in the mirror, nimbus brilliance. outside her

door, his sandpaper hands down his pants.
why his grunts still startle us, after all this time:
quiet, a phantom limb, its itching quite unbearable.

even now, amputation's romance. she lays
to rest our missing pieces, tucks them in,
and whispers a prayer. on the ninth day,

novena. on the fortieth day, rosary, offered
to the patron saint against solitary death.
with such elegance, these forlorn gestures.

the door, pulled from its hinges.

dear love,

today i am through with your surface acts of contrition, i am through
witnessing your mimicry of prescribed other, your fervor for the
part. your self-damnation for your fervor. dear cycle of transgression
and redemption, for that is what you are, dear love, godless, but for
tokens, honorary titles, footnotes in their dust covered tomes. once,
even up until yesterday, my compassion for you, the tenderness of our
peripheral geographies, seduced me. i wanted so much this kinship
for which you feign indifference. i am through with your parades
and affectations, your self-damnation for your feigning, your survival
rationale mass appeal. i can no longer bear the sight of you paid but
not recompensed, claimed, theirs. i swore i loved you once. but now
i have grown w(e)ary. dear love, i too am culpable, perhaps i am even
uncivil, but i can no longer honor you.

and then there is tomorrow, dear promise, dear mirror, to test my skin
with your forked tongue.

(ā'zhə, fĭl)

n.

1. A non-Asian male who prefers Asian women. This preference is based upon media stereotypes of Asian women, whom he believes are more gratifying sexual partners.

2. A white western male with a pathological, sexual obsession with Asians and their cultures.

3. A non-Asian person, most often a white male, with yellow fever*.

4. A white male with a sexual interest in Asian cultures and Asian women.

5. A non-Asian male who browses Asian porn sites and has a secret Asian porn collection. He frequents bible studies, Asian oriented message boards. In colleges, he is found in Asian Studies courses, learning an Asian language.

He believes Asians are "beautiful," "polite," and "agreeable." Despite this admiration, he addresses them in patronizing, condescending tones that he does not speak to Caucasians.

The more advanced of his kind travels to Asia, historically for purposes of war, and in contemporary settings, "to teach English," "to complete a doctoral thesis," "to collect art(ifacts)." There, he patronizes brothels and massage parlors. There, he purchases his Asian wife, spawns biracial children, and soon divorces, before the bruises disappear, after the restraining orders.

*Yellow Fever is also called Black Vomit or sometimes the American Plague.

[she prays to san miguel arcángel]

¿dónde está el camino de realidad?

o prince of the heavenly host, to thee we pray
for deliverance. be our defense against
the devil, his snares, his dazzling darkness,
his love for the ruin of our humble souls.

she lifts her shot glass above her head,
toasts heaven, drives spirit down the gullet.
she will continue to do this until the demons
circling her disappear into church walls.
until the bottle is an empty nest of shards.

perdición de las almas.

heaps of skeletons buried without ceremony
push through the floorboards and gasp for air.

[evidence]

grandpa fisherman oversees the suturing:
fishtails to primate torsos, post-mortem.
materials include fishbone needles,

human hair, pincher ants' mandibles.
sprinkling crystallized salts to desiccate,
his hands dance in fish-cleaning manner.

the art, grandpa says, is in matching
the corpses. to suture is to fix a hole.
trashy talismans bring dollars to tip jars.

[the siren's story]

she wasn't born in this city. she found its basalt greenstone chunks,
seafloor forced skyward. it found her hands through mist and odors
whirring pigeons' clubfeet fluttering, toothless men's paper sacks
spilling elixirs, roots, shark fin tonics. heat swelling sewer steam
rising, side street chess match maneuvers mystifying. it sought her
whirlwind hair, grown seavine thick. songbird, adrift, nestling neon,
she crafted snares for moths, butterflies, treasure hunting children
tracing ideographs: sky, sun. patina spires, smirking dragon boys
humming silk lanterns, flight of phoenixes through fish vendors'
stalls, corrugated plastic blackbird perches, jade-ringed gardens,
needle-tipped shanties. it bulleted trees, lighting hash pipes;
herbalists' storefront canopies concealing leathered men, versed in
languages of whiskered ghosts. it invented her dialect carving tongue:
salt fables, yellow caution tape palaces. she lost herself in this city.
it lured her, drank her air; honey voice's precision, hybrid beyond
memory. songbird, adrift, this city's misplaced siren. migration
patterns subterranean streams swallowed whole.

dear love, i touched the bamboo cage today i dreamt your body inside
of it persecuted upright. the thing about bamboo it is supposed to
bend to one's will bound with wild grasses it embraces a man's body
allows his subtle aspirations he must sleep upright during typhoon
season he would drown otherwise he sleeps cicada lullaby and he
forgets he is a prisoner of godless places

dear love, i touched the bamboo cage today remembered malakas
and maganda tapping from inside the pliant stalk emerging from its
splintered form bathala sent the bird into the world she heard a noise
lipad maya dagat araw mar y sol shouting rocks and wind

i am confusing my creation stories but my point is these prisons must
contain might and beauty storytellers have told me so much depends
upon my believing them

[panambitan]

forgive, forgive, for principles won't do. river's thralls of strange
witchcraft and the breaking strain of ships. you have angered the
evil spirits of the machine, and they demand appeasement. this is
why you have come, a man presenting himself as a voice, always
suspecting the jungle's eyes are not human. if they are, capable of
humanity, then they are the first men, wordless, taking possession
of accursed inheritance. no, you wish for deliberate belief. you insist
upon absolution and deliverance. and so it shall be.

[zoetrope]

he appears a singular figure through slits. cinematic wisdom humility.
he is moral battle mad. he endeavors metaphoric. he is genre jungle.
horror classic. psychodrama supplant. vietnam kick. he is rich richer
epic sublime. masterpiece embellish. he is monumental deletion
satisfying. he indulges broken sinew. he undercuts sociopolitical
astonishment. his backbone is stalinist correction. he sees opportunity
imagistic microcosm. he is episodic sprawl. his glory reasonable
genius. he is numbing diatribe. big nothing unscripted. he is
conducive to corpulence. he is insane in the monsoon rain. he is
a posse of errand boys, hapless assassins. he lives on this street. he
complicates cardiac arrest: the blood, the booze, the glass are real.
he is the set, the new cut, both inferior but great. he is 14-year
old gunner launching. he is industry loving vietnam boy coming
of age war. his wishful fantasy, his streets, his guilt-laden academy
loves vietnam headtrips and phantasms singing. his invaders' blues
narratives spinning. central axis creating illusion of movement. he
is insanity defense plea. he banks philippine beach bitch cheap. his
convenience shadow. he exacts disposable penance stand-ins. he is
megalomaniac directing fear, scattering frantic peasants. he is celluloid
persuasion syndrome. he is disease of obscured etiology.

he knows that american kids who kill die without a clue without
subtitles to know if their victims begged for mercy with voices dubbed
over their own. but with military vehicles rented from martial law
dictator he conspires with indelicate savage. he is that which appears

natural mechanical process. though light source is not critical there is
a love story here struggling to show itself.

thigh deep in rice paddy sludge, a trapped wife testifies, prays she
does not contract malaria the next time he abandons her here.
malnutrition has rendered her pliant body now the frame of a teenage
whore. clavicle, ribcage protrusions. a robust man, he could shatter
her pelvis with a thoughtless thrust. she dreams of shopping sprees in
tokyo, in hong kong. about her ankles and knees, mud-blind tilapia
and catfish lay eggs and remember rivers.

dear love,

you dream in the language of dodging bullets and artillery fire.
new, sexy diagnoses have been added to the lexicon on your behalf
("charlie don't surf," has also been added to the lexicon on your behalf).

in this home that is not our home, we have mutually exiled each
other. i walk down your street in the rain, and i do not call you. i
walk in the opposite direction of where i know to find you. that we
do not speak is louder than bombs.

there are times that missing you is a matter of procedure. now is
not one of those times. there are times when missing you hurts. so
it comes to this, vying for geography. there is a prayer stuck in my
throat. douse me in gasoline, my love, and strike a match. let's see
this prayer ignite to high heaven.

[elegy for the colonel]

i have known moons, the darkest pearls.

luminous one, he knew the myth,
how morningstar fell from grace.
his mother's airy lullabies, scarred wings aflutter.

he knew eclipses, a beast swallowing sky,
a predator guided by busted streetlights.
where sirens made their gutter homes,
where crickets made symphony halls of dumpsters,
where rust chain fences ringed jagged playgrounds,

such radiance, pure
moonlight, he always believed.

he knew jungles, once baptized godless people.
hazel-eyed children of soldiers and warbride waifs
drowned in rivers, tender ankles he roped to stone.
he learned bloodletting to appease demons.
with every bullet, libation to the soul stealer.

elders say, a skilled hunter inhabits his prey's soul.
a man who forsook his stars, consumed by his own
body's missing pieces. he cradled single perspiration beads,
dewdrop gems in his palms. every part, every precious part.
he waltzed with parking meters, he shooed away onlookers.

elders say he died of lunacy.

now sleep, and let salt water corrode your place of rest.
sleep, dear one, and let the darkest pearls fill this city's open mouth.

[agimat kinabukasan]

one day she will build a temple from detritus, dust of your
crumbling empires' edicts; its walls will hold with blood and spittle,
brackish water and sun-dried grasses. within these walls she will
inscribe her own terms of worship, upon every pillar and column,
glyphs resembling earth and ocean. once she had no sharpened
stone, no reason for stone, for once the wind bore her words upon
its entire wingspan. carved into bamboo, banana leaf, her river
poems, her birdsong.

you came then, with your devices, and you will come again, believing
yourself to be some cipher, some illuminati, plunder-hungry in
secrecy. she will not appease you, but with the fire you once took to
her flesh, she will melt down your weapons, forge her own gods, and
adorn her own body.

it is for no glory, no father, no doctrine. as it was in the beginning, so
shall it be again. in plumes of ash blanketing sky, the land expels that
with which she was poisoned.

[panalanging sigaw]

panaginip lamang ang itong dakilang lunsod, ari-arian daw ng
mga dayuhang mandarambong at mandarahas. ang mga daan ay
napupuno ng manlulupig, kristyanong may malaking baril, at isang
napakatinong bingi't pipi. walang nakikinig sa kaniyang sigaw.

nguni't laging alalahain namin: itong lunsod ng panaginip ay
pagkaligaw sa tunay. pag lumuluha ang lupa, dumadalisay na apoy
ang mga luha niya. pag may bagyo, sumisigaw ang lupa. ang sabi
niya: tama na.

hindi alang-alang sa luwalhati, sa diyos, sa doktrina. ang sa simula ay
magiging na naman. ikinukubli ng kalangitan ang mga ulap ng abo,
pinapaalis ng lupa ang lason.

�574ᓂᕆᔭᑯᒋ ᐁᖓᑭ

ᓚᕐᒥᔭᐅᑦ ᐊᓂᔭ ᓲᕆ ᒐᖃᔨᑦ ᐸᓐᒍ ᓘᕙᕐᓘᕆ ᒥ ᓃ ᔭᓲᒃ ᒐᓯᕿ ᕐᒐᒐᒐᑕ ᕆ ᓴᒡᔭᒥ �II
ᕆ ᔭᓴᕆ ᒐᓕ ᕆ ᑎᓂᕆᑦᓂ ᓂ ᕆᑎᒋᓂ ᐊᒪᓲᓂ ᑦ ᕆᑎᒃᑖ ᐊᑯᐊ ᕆ ᓲᐅ ᑎᓂᓃᕆᕆᓂ ᐊᓕᓲ
ᓘᓃ II ᐱᓂ ᓴᖅᐊᔨ ᕆ ᐸᑭᓚᕝ ᐁᖓᑭ

ᔭᕐᓂ ᐱᔨ ᕆᑎᓱᓲᖅ ᓂᐅ II ᓲᕆ ᑦᐁ ᓂ ᓚᕐᒥᔭᓪ ᕆ ᓴᖅᑖᔨ ᐁ ᕆᑎ II ᓂᕆ ᑦᐅᕆᕆ ᕆ
ᑦᓂᕆ ᒐᐅᒥᑦᐁ ᓂ ᕆᕆᑦ ᕆ ᔭᓴᕆ ᑦᕆᕆ ᕿᓂᕆ II ᓂᕆ ᕆ ᐊᐅᕆ ᐁᑭᐊᐁᔨ ᕆ ᑦᓂᕆ II ᕆ ᐁᐊ
ᕿᓂᕆ ᕆᕐᕆ ᓂ

ᓱᒃ ᕆᑦᕆᑦ ᐁ ᑦᓴᓱᕆ ᐁ ᕿᑭᐁ ᐁ ᕿᕐᓂᐁ II ᕆ ᐁ ᐁᐁᕆᑦ ᕆ ᕐᔨᔨ ᓂ ᓂᕆ II
ᒐᖃᓂᕝᑦ ᓂ ᒐᑦᔮᕆ ᕆ ᔭᓲᒋ ᔭᕆ ᓂ ᕆᐊ ᓃᑎᓂᕆᕝ ᓂ ᑦᓂᕆ ᕆ ᑦᐁ

[A Woman Asks]

Don't I pray God perched vulgar and dire
Don't accidents carry sovereign fire
Why desire altered chain schemata or mores
Sickened skill neglects poseurs ill versed entire
Undulate prescience culled nonsense choir
Perched no sparrows come to debase your chorus
Atoll raging on poor innocents
Caged senses natural this monstrous
None of talents devolve or prove our
Love's nascence killed farcical hour
We quell each swallowed virtue each swallow of penance
Lessons the poetical son's movement decrescendos
Pieced mementos jailed fathers amorous
As seers honed pervade interlopers monstrous

Equaled ports do veil memorial
Pretenders' statues sea formation chromed
Dear fondled looming do not surely tawdry
Like quality art in vain for the menial
Elegy we create each sensation numbed
Their alms consumed the choral volatility
Fiend's vendetta firmament intention
Shall pretension nil possible stilettos
Show me instant ghettos' glocked demoralization
Unequal parts of my non-possession
Forget the quality of non-decisions
Resplendence insists perpetual effects
None a dilettante's mere considerate stanzas
For caged impotent liars simile glances

[lakas sambayan 2003]

stone torch in nation's fist fractures

dictator's face wings flutter yellow paint

streaming from this giant's lachrymal ducts

inventoried war crimes swiss bank accounts

dialysis paparazzi copycats bless american way

iron tanks cannot deter nuns wailing

novenas guarding ballot boxes with rosaries

remember the agong as woman's breast

remember generala silang brandishing bolo knife

riding bareback where confluence of fishmarket

freeways prefab housing squares meet basketball

courts liquor stores cornrowed b-ballers sport

saggin sean john bling bling knuckles

lowering rice rockets scraping tha pavement

vinta colors billow island monsoon sky

street chrome exhaust pipes black smoke

pimpin boyz flip they caps sideways

faraway spectacle this commissioned stone face

no rushmore mere quick dry cement

block amnesia exile nation cannot dismantle

Confession(al)

Forgive me father, for here have I faltered.
It has been thirty years and counting,
the process of my acculturation.

A pure product of America, my English
is more proficient than many native speakers;
usage conventions and colloquialisms do not elude

me. I have no accent to affect, though I have
often contemplated acquiring one. Father, have you
ever heard of a coconut? This is the best metaphor

for me. I have often contemplated acquiring
an authenticity marker, a lovely affect:
Diwa Kayumanggi Maharlika Makata.

For the names I have been given:
Hispanic Hussy! Slanty-eyed Ho!
cannot bind one to any one place:

Los Angeles Mexico City
Hong Kong Hanoi Bangkok
San Juan Havana Madrid

Manila.
San Francisco.
And even more.

[Filipino Names]

Our waiter in the pizza joint is Jhay-Pee.
The bartender at the Watering Hole is Rhey.
The boy I kiss there is Alexis. He has a Batman tattoo,
Drinks Johnny Lumalakad on the rocks, and I drink rhum.
The boys in the cover band are Rocky, Hazel, and Ichiban.
Ichiban has no fingers on his right hand.
Hazel's got big eyes and jacked up teeth. It's kind of sexy.

In Cagayan, we party with Aloc, Bembol, Darius, Aries, Dodo.
Aloc and Darius stuff us in a tricycle and take us to a cockfight.
We are the only girls there. Feedie, nicknamed Bembol,
With his up to no good, licking his chops, cocking his eyebrow smile,
Smokes in church, daring me to do the same.
Late night drinking gin, sitting so close his vibe is electric; lighting
My cigarette a good enough reason to stare hard into my eyes.
Not to be mistaken for Frederick, Aloc is Federick,
Feedie's younger brother who crosses himself
With holy water, genuflecting at the church entryway;
A gentleman, walking two steps behind us,
Chaperoned by Tita Beng, Fleur de Lis, and Manang Inday
For a perfect countryside stroll after last night's rain.

In Manila, my Tita Tin's insanely cute driver is Bong.
We don't know what that's short for.
Our own cousin Bong is short for Ludevico.
We don't know where that came from either.

Shieljeh's big bro Shiegfield's baby is Rudensfeld.

Cousin Johnny Adviento is Butchoy;

Tito Doming the sea captain is Dominador,

And Gerardo Salvador Lantoria III, MD,

Former lead guitarist of the metal band Leper Messiah,

Is, and always shall be Thirdyboy.

Uncle Darlac from Marikina doesn't say much,

So I don't know what else to say about him.

Manang Ambat's granddaughter GE

Does not stand for General Electric.

But no one can tell us her real name.

[lullaby in SoMa for paloma]

rhapsodist of mission street, she knows symphonies of human
skull to parking meter collisions, where crystal meth boys in
go-go boots don't know today from next week, and bloodshot
men are an itch in her sock. she tumbles down someplace hotel
stairs, braids flying behind her turf tag blur hallways bounding
between galaxies, following the rattle of amber vials' pink pills
click-shake-swallow-swig. puka shell boys and dredlock brothas
roll phat blunts, shadows behind telephone poles shiftshaping
into fire hydrants. paloma bathes in streetcleaners' antibacterial
rivulets, scavenges cigarette butts from sidewalk crevices, tucks
them beneath her wings for future reference. mission street
rhapsodist, she remembers mineral soaks could remove her
fishscales to make her resemble a woman dreaming of french
manicures, spa soap, lorca proselytizing lithium clouds, dirges,
expiration dates, buildings edged with scratch and fire escapes.
she tumbles down someplace between this planet and the next,
there is atmosphere to lighten her lungs to burst into flames.
how many days will it take to walk to the sky? she's packed
provisions she doesn't know how to count — licorice root, peyote,
henna, tobacco sack, whiskey flask, tea leaves for warpath ghosts.
skeptics truck driving coyotes shards of strangers' confessions,
sound of fallen mango, no inventory of color, no measure of
objects' worth; a vulture's talon, some keepsake sister of
morning dew in languages of other times — rot silk fishbones.
city limits always receding and receding with sunset sweetness.

[epilogue]

[on viewing subjective catastrophe]

what i can see: an archangel's wings. birdsong. a melting popsicle. a game of hopscotch. a robin's breast. a blood orange. an aurora framed in sunset.

this one tiny corner's rose petals to ease my eyes.

(he asks me to translate.) (the tongue of an angry man.) (he tells me, i don't know how i feel about this.) (any of this?) (i want to grab his shoulders and shake.) (jesus, feel something.) (he walks away.) (he can't hear me.) (he smiles.)

do you know what it is to witness an unraveling? it is being at the right place at the wrong time, or being at the wrong place at the right time. both may break you.

think.

wanna peek into my notebook? there may be clues hidden in it: instructions for viewing subjective catastrophe. rules of derivation. don't gasp. don't choke. up. look up. cradle your neck from holding the gaze.

keep your eyes to the sky and think of heaven.

[puso]
joey ayala sings 16 lovesongs

consider this a mythology
a faith you hold in a sieve
a salt cave a veil of ghazal

i dream a tar-hued
salamander dotted
tangerine slinking
up bedroom walls

i dream a grotto
of saints and starlight

i open my eyes
an iridescence
of mothwings

precision of rhapsody
in my father's tongue
a mermaid of emerald
oceans bantering
midnight moontide

dislodge these words
from my throat
with a single breath —

ugat.

lupa.

halik.

sayaw.

dugo.

ligtas.

ulap.

lipad.

langit.

umaga.

ligaya.

bituin.

buwan.

diwa.

ginhawa.

awit.

dapat ganito ang pag-ibig:

tunay,

tunay.

"If William Blake were alive and well and sitting on a eucalyptus branch in the hills above the bay, this is the poetry he would aspire to write."
—*James Longenbach*

Barbara Jane Reyes was born in Manila, Philippines and raised in the San Francisco Bay Area. She received her undergraduate education at UC Berkeley and her MFA in Creative Writing (poetry) at SF State University. Her first book, *Gravities of Center,* was published by Arkipelago Books (San Francisco) in 2003.

Her work was recently nominated for a Pushcart Prize, and appears or is forthcoming in *Asian Pacific American Journal, Chain, Interlope, Nocturnes (Re)view, North American Review, Tinfish, Versal,* in the anthologies *Babaylan* (Aunt Lute, 2000), *Eros Pinoy* (Anvil, 2001), *Going Home to a Landscape* (Calyx, 2003), *Not Home But Here* (Anvil, 2003), *Pinoy Poetics* (Meritage, 2004), *Graphic Poetry* (Hong Kong: Victionary, 2005), and forthcoming in *Red Light: Superheroes, Saints and Sluts* (Vancouver: Arsenal Pulp, 2005).